Encroach to Resume

Also by Peter Larkin

Enclosures
Prose Woods
Pastoral Advert
Terrain Seed Scarcity
Slights Agreeing Trees
Sprout Near Severing Close
Rings Resting The Circuit
What the Surfaces Enclave of Wang Wei
Leaves of Field *
Lessways Least Scarce Among *
Imparkments (The Surrogate Has Settled)
Give Forest Its Next Portent *
City Trappings (Housing Heath or Wood)
Introgression Latewood *
Trees Before Abstinent Ground *

Wordsworth and Coleridge: Promising Losses

* *Titles from Shearsman Books*

Peter Larkin

Encroach to Resume

Shearsman Books

First published in the United Kingdom in 2021 by
Shearsman Books Ltd
PO Box 4239
Swindon
SN3 9FN

Shearsman Books Ltd Registered Office
30–31 St. James Place, Mangotsfield, Bristol BS16 9JB
(this address not for correspondence)

www.shearsman.com

ISBN 978-1-84861-756-8

Copyright © Peter Larkin, 2021.

The right of Peter Larkin to be identified as the author
of this work has been asserted by him in accordance with the
Copyrights, Designs and Patents Act of 1988.
All rights reserved.

ACKNOWLEDGEMENTS

Grateful thanks to the following magazines and their editors where extracts from some of these poems first appeared: *The Fortnightly Review, Junction Box, Litter, Plumwood Mountain, Shearsman magazine, SNOW.*

It's also a pleasure to thank Tony Frazer once again for all his support at Shearsman.

Contents

Roots on Foot /
Feet in Root

7

Spaces || in the way
of Forest

27

As a Tree
Not a Tree

39

Given Trees Their
Other Side of Nature

59

Skies in
Flight of Tree

73

Bodies
the Trees of

87

Snag of
a Tree

95

The unicity of the visible world, and, by encroachment, the invisible world … is the solution of the problems of the 'relations between the soul and the body'. (VI,233)

Flesh of the world, described… as segregation, dimensionality, continuation, latency, encroachment. (VI, 248)

My personal life must be the resumption of a prepersonal tradition. There is… another subject beneath me, for whom the world exists before I am here, and who marks out my place in it. (PP, 254)

Sensation, as the primordial contact with being, is the resumption…of a form of existence, itself constitutive of a setting for co-existence, of a space (PP, 255)

—Maurice Merleau-Ponty

ROOTS ON FOOT
/ FEET IN ROOT

1987 (2018)

For Bruce Andrews

Note

The present text is a heavily edited and partly re-written version of a long poem simply called 'roots/ /feet' written between 1986–7 but which was never published. It arose from a trenchant saying I came across by Bruce Andrews, something like 'why bother with roots when all we need is feet?' I felt a need to regurgitate, experiment and tussle with this, and I think there is still some life in the material though perhaps the immediate context has gone.

January, 2018

He walks still upright with the Root
Meas'ring the Timber with his Foot
    ANDREW MARVELL

Huge roots intertwin'd
With wildest texture
    COLERIDGE

that it provides 'feet' for thought…
It is, in short, less radical. 'Where are human feet?'
    GEOFFREY HARTMAN

I

the insatiability of meaning it not rooted, were feet
wearied, not weaned   not footing placing but
peculiar putting

            to disexemplify (a root) the interruption
of repose erupts it only foot-height

                        but origin is imper-
ative, the then start: sharpest rejoinders before universal
inclination

            cleft-referee: divide the feet on which a root
frets   foot-skill in itinerary, the latter adds
root-sheet, a kernel elongated (footlike) and reducible

            bare feet close the envelope of flaps, root
no breeze felt   what aspect of the body's inertia defies
feet their root-shape?   the passage through has no
replacement feet can unfold

'cutting nature at the joints a root delusion'   the surf-
ace a stream on jointed limb, root in striding-own missed
prison   soonness of feet ought not to be idle within
the paring of root

                foot-level because slung over roots,
no barrier-free exterior sign, the streams of root bushed
on the footway   regional-essential whereby clos-
ure a detour if it endure, sealed ornate (a little) but
rarely other enough a site of deployables

                    what regulars of
sect where the roots crawl under the horizon, an
exclave, swathing the feet against this cut of steps?
roots drift, feet omit?   use the rail to a room and
a half (half as of each foot) the ego of roots   feet
shorter to go

                                      spray
ground at root-collapse (siphon across the hollow) smears
sole the thin-won feet   inherent in the floor disgulfs
the basic, put roots an everywhere inherently not a mom-
ent of rest at the footpoint's re-posed

                            to stay overlong
underground strips distance of immediate overlay, far
cast, not spreading belief but stepping on it needed, to
avoid the overlay (roots lacing over the feet) the main
limit must be holed up in inherent move

the floor roots lie on, stand, not open

the door feet tie on, alone again erect   the
wafer on the lip of the feet

                flattening an open world
                pressed-roots of rehearsals

II–III

feet   dubiety
of binding function

roots   the
agentless step

feet can't put mosaic,
sooner stretch root
higher an amount,
pluck it off thudless
deep, each knock
absorbs a common head

roots may be subheadings
theirs to looseners
below no apex
counter-normal tenacity
an essential egress unheaded

at the end of something
inimitable stalk they
repent on. Either repost
or unincludeds an effacive
omission no bed else
supports, the feet
damage, ahead and behind
is so laced
back in limb

classes in nature, classes
in-striding, risens
in feet rooted to disposal
but kick under
the frequent prepersists
and nearer concealable over,
dead immunity foot
to foot the roots can't
trail, unforbidden
stays for a loosened

beyond fallaway
go walking-omit
deport 'extraneous poise'
wade off glues
no shatterfoot

that must be broken,
that evades site of the
inseparable stroke, that
everything can isn't
skipped, the shatter
ramification so

what use of feet
given non-parallelism of time
over earth's two-way ridden? in
class to remotely lost
exits feet mayn't stack
one rejector above another

feet not as pegs
whose roots don't
apprentice longitude, an
interval lain
since mobile apart

miniature cyst-in
(sy)stem a spine accelerates
to blunt govern by feet.

feet, the interstices
of their own, defray
the rootsearch of it

foot to print (alarmer)
no direct touch, screen
a leaf on the plain
if to walk along its laid
state (outer rider) unless
deep extended real

feet over roots seek no
season of enthusiasm,
not thinly prone

ill-posed to accords of risk,
feet wish not demountable
conduction reveres
poor little trot of earth

feet desire to vouch
earth after so much
inclusion-fatigue range,
a recession procedure
left to sink
beckoning trapped by the feet,
no commentary on the captivity

its trape an opener
overly independent-closed,
provides skipping in dearth
of sift, death with the root in

don't strike this away
because no attribution
in not stretching the surface
as if root would not
be outdwarfed

a time to rebody
but stepped at door
the current now keen
drawn beyond remnant

root out the hole
now for unsecret fork
the shadow moves to
whither load?

a sudden deceleration
obliges: to overstep

high as root stemmed
in the further braking?

thus feet may fear infect-
ion threads, roots too pre-
mature (*ie* antiunraisable)

feet graft distance
split by pace
arch via root
what root number
on myriad feet
to be bound?
to nowhere but feet
bringing a geni-
dentical bite
solace instep

injury feet, by
root node
noisy interpretation

overherding the link
but not how they run
schemeless
late disinterrance

pushed or shown extent
as thinned root, no deal-
ings the banter of ground
drawn to feet

issue a series of rivals,
series in step outright
support, the contest
heals the mouth of issue

the aporia *is* paths, in
roots of, porous impasse,
its infatuations shorn
of possible led past
but are ranker let

thickening into pools
else tapering off: these
cease volition once
(bounce) foot-thrown

beddings kill for rooting,
footings fill before trodden

truth the island can touch
ensandment, expose
to close, roots graver
from both sides

no given plummet ought revert,
no abyss *before* root

underground crowded
against concourse, not
'undertaking nativeness'

roots reach a table of
self-cancellation
however the notch-up (surface)
is unburdened with supply

roots have no back on
which to be trodden
key up but turning,
counter-erect as the very foot

roots permit no ground of pursuit

they ceded their pre-
for long as far over

pin to feet upright behind
a back 'going on' a
pause of fact, foot burier
the roots' junior body?

the abyss in the fold, go along
if root is wedged by its
counter-revival, an empty
function pleased (puts
beside) reserve

the angle at which it retorts
no longer its own parting
since feet never ascended

they begin to sink less object,
terror but no brink

foot-finished regress (*not*
foot sampled) released but
below where it radiates
under the stamping out.

root-disputants no
mutants, to desist
giving out the grip

burdens apply, steal effect
as of no leaving cure

no extra quota of root, bad
double of feet

IV

A querulous avenue from below, final amounts. Joint-bound to imagery above ground but only the one type got there (ankle). The busied object's made-possible version so to settle out, its street-level had been mostly root-level. From armature to nature, from discard to kick-off. If a way to a step, enhancements making way are disliked, the liminal of this separation isn't steep but unspaciously erect. The feet can't rival one another, nor insulate being singled along by whichever trail takes them. Nothing if not a foot upon that, flat to a fall which can't plunge or tail.

Horizon (reckoned below surface) concedes an instep arch, this will truck through flat effects devised by a super-trail swirl, the erect tipping-up. Any dwelling pulls the site out of you, onto the feet used to, root-surplus of spaces off goal. Smaller and smaller systems of overcome aridity to stain the area.

No bulge between feet and roots, come flatten against an ahead. The hollow of it at best overhead (upright), the gap can't be less than press flat-out across the plain. Continuity is points planning particular rhythms for shortest paths, but widely dominated by like distance-to-step. The dead-end is some turn like this forbidden repetition on which it sparks gridless (that it could only turn). Mobile roots do increase steps where they are, at every outlet a plan taken on foot, site specific exile delivery. Free-grounding archaic roots hardly akin to any rotating model are as much feet as can't walk the rounds. These straighten up having been tided over, simple-undulate. Feet will collapse but not vertically, the 'standing' knows many grassings, all of which are simple at laying over root. It would be innocent to enscarce back to root which the foot cordons, falling in but not grouping. Erect foot lateralises counter to overflowing root. This is reconcilable but not awardable, any co-homology already aggressed by walking on. By which the stalk on which the foot sweeps was but overgrown root, segments snatch the pivot but work it vertically into the use of trail. Roots were above flight, until their ramification staged a filter from the wings. No base substitute were not feet rigid with unnecessary choice, movable-static apart mobile-bound.

Avoid feet where roots become overt, but as there are no interstices (steps to) without fixation, it's that which keeps them coming on. The trail by which we seem to brush it down to an equivalent is a released apex structure, lateral-hoverable treks. So a major discarded system (roots) traduces the minor discards, snouts of passage. As void considered independent for *external* obstacles only, not itself a free frame of. The function could only be absolute by switching (laying the roots over) whatever distributes the search horizon more than it estimates the stance. Roots stretch and it is roots which snapped through, 'from the centre' is ghostly anger returning, to its unscanty houseless dots where a break might have been all well, but feet can't allow for such a cross-section: their rigid-erect splits along the rod they are two of. Reciprocity is an element separation, an image that combs the same pattern to a number of likings. Each layer thin enough to erect plan against fork, not leave itself only 'living out the means' as pure flow.

Not didacticism of feet but ventilation of root: the same recipe in one place or another, erect or flat but efficiently (the feet do move) not the former place. The same course? Sufficient to invite roots not to part with this ride of it.

The pinned cavity itself streams the movement out of subspace, were it not root bated us. Drawing the feet, inner effect completely relative to its measure out of, fears most. A gantry around the mark of the footfall which becomes apparent intersection (coded repeat space) or a blatant root-tuning. Roots can't flex at anything field-like, role-change is merely strewn across them, kicked to settle by any source of earth raising its feet.

If not transfer-fragile at their separate holds, the looming feet stitch the spreading roots at a prime come-out (root first) only ever offered to next burdens (which the trail so far hasn't relived). As if this were a slice across horizon whose edges should loom up vertically and target a next close-down or next nearly-on again. Bi-criterion network, yes, but the paths are only multiple in the easing shape of what speckles usable roots, dusting them step by step. Feet the alias of variance, replicas by simply aligning one ramification over another, and rendering unlightly onward their resort to fork.

V

    the 'existed empties'   never rests abroad no matter
    how sufficient the pace takes place,   *ie* long going by known unit
    off the scale of its force   less this to imprint for
    density than able to foot it strictly down   the lack of
    infliction accepted

                      out of root were feet but to get along
any present stage, but it opens a shepherding cycle, not graded
from flock so feet didn't trestle   were they merely directed smooth
as a hare to form?

                what allies if not smoothings a foot makes
quake   to crush the fruit at once or get underway,
unseen spores enrol steps about a hugging globe?

if the level is unrounded (tread), moving away is not entered by
whatever would so begin, even given away, but will be carried,
not deposited, around any partial load   the premium to move
(primum mobile) goes along root-escape   a smoothness foot-
figments it, has infinite room to be borne   feet never
put forth without brushing the combs they co-figure a trail by,
sandily intromittent, rake up the pace

                            the intervals (less
vacuum) keep it with themselves but rival barwise for fear of
an emergence   that any one step extend a population, not
another step

    root-theres or any two of two   plural but not shallow stride it
    offpaid the adjusts   in as much no 'get-at' would
    couple pace as lengthening 'the wedge'
                            underwing some unpleat-
    ing spreadprint or smoothstone   this shadowing hierarchy

proffers a more than flout-easy ex-lost at base   repeats were
easily planed, not deftly packed

array on/off   each climate switched at fixed because
so little 'at'   neither is it like an unjust conduction, not having
chipped even a divot from the land-bridge over roots   wholly
that disprisoning as if for an emergence at all gates ahead

off/on slash aroot   lean it simply smooth off the vertical as
it does on a foot's beat   nothing thins unenchanceable touch
but what will beat bounds *from* touch   each is taken to as for steps
must be   part of the shell of glacial flatness *is* unbroken,
whatever make-way there is in shifting over   a radiance etiolates
far flung its below-raids cradle the gates

                                a secretary cell transect
cuts flatness to limb, hardly sedentary, does divide on but do not lay it
so, will avoid arrival clusters ground to foot   no lived lines
could be flatter save a slight undulation not *owing* feet   and no
kicking the mark across from that unburied cycle without a root's own
rotation

    nature such traceism without jargon

    how smooth feet are when not tending the roots' tremble

    strew underreach whose rhythm isn't racing them

VI

To walk away entire were it not for the surfacing. Not engulfed in stasis but as much on a level with it. The foot merely holds to surface the roots' crawl they didn't take. Even though roots had never been a fill-in, no plain thing is simply above them. Much paradigm assumes effusion, capillary trash flattened but stalk-easy. In racks at shock of bed, bedding crash away. Whatever medial spaces are daunted laterally.

Feet circle not roots but a pre-amplitude any-neglect lateral. The command-spills: an infinite sub-fit dangerously near starts a super-trace surface. As feet have no spreader technique, they sink at root but not to flourish there with their scuffing. How literal a plantar a scarcely flexed overlay compellent. No massage to ramification other than the earth-shell itself not yet completely outward. Just now unsealed-inert imputes a plain face to the contiguity.

Not amiss and not situated, out of point onto dune. Otherwise, roots have no abrasion from privilege, the dislodgement is a common horizontal. But in its properties not directing effect. Root bares this, the contamination apprises exposure. So, no sensation setting away with, stepping off. Lazy prints, however, sometimes leave the root-droppings coveted. Such a throughness as has had to, a real stir to lateral span.

What enticements to depart universally could feet now understand? Never erect enough themselves to have known correction. It's what the unsent roots have exactly never done, to *rest* on the plain as needn't provoke a pause. Is it enough to have forfeit of the hold now in disrelief? A ranging above ground, exemption of ground excepted. Feet only variable dependents as a little against immersion. Walk out at any time staunchly wider, less a steep. No possibility of walking *up* the root.

Roots not traced to any itinerary. Keeping roots below what they radiate as though trodden out. This is just what can't be struck once the roots fatten up to surface. No weight is thrown around in the passive-undisplaced.

Critical uppermost at restricted channel until mantled in a lateral planet. Its own induced monopitch imagines feet are 'dropped onto'. No secret surface that there's a shaft to landing. If roots, longer and longer, no longer set hurdles on that sort of rank. The postface huddle community, to find it not beckoning them aside. 'Processual paradigms' arrive governing the intersection. Couplings as the amplitude worsens but loosens whatever asymmetry took sides with a come-along apparatus it could almost resemble.

A lateral prowess of uprights underpinning, *ie* feet can't be matched flush to surface anymore than roots don't cease protruding. A lateral system is not what to excuse from untethereds, but upon which side of the projecting root does it pass? Such steady potential in shift is vantage-correct at least, but roots through it don't keep in true their scrounge-effect. There's no basis for steering the equivalent. Roots in retroset whose decks effect a vast over-learning by foot. Stands selective to base liberation, given it would merely have surpassed this from below. Walks out as far as the hinter-universal patterned for, of basal blessing.

To develop when to be puzzled, to be clumsy, the width in such open case (visible root) is upward still. As if verticalizing the curve of margin where its turn climbs ever under you. Erect into the trace itself could the stretchless plain really be that unneedy. But the wide is readily alongside, the feet only stand on a single length twice in a while.

No rest apart as planes. Hierarchies crew the impossible end, as technically assigning them. Roots have no careful resolve apart from this semi-skill. Arches of the step now calmer from an ominous-

generous interior, but onto solo danger as affronting base level. Consider how little surface the upright foot ever buries. Almost perfect on a touch used as the little of the move. It's possible ankle-bones are roots straight out (vertical with exit) behoving the illusion of movement much as losing itself.

Ipsilaterally oppresses the fount, will out, but rarely free so ulterior a bundle. There are no one-mover construction tasks. In shipping the roots we sag between them our nearer snagging. No *lateral* vastness following the under-stiffnesses once that is where they want to soften surplus foundation. No horizontal armature, lateral kindness is not one of compliance unless the roots *protrude* what they desist.

Rigid verticals may not even reside aslant since feet are new to any take-out. The surface slips and sucks at its spears. Scarce novation of step and no fresh shuttle material for the alliance. Support offers to a non-homogenous, the original *must* expect a uniform sunken aspect, unsnubbed. Rapidly shredded along. For which the only partner is nearest wave-crush, a torrent of root of which the crest (tested) gets on its feet.

VII

weaken a root genuine
step if it augment its
applicability. What can
apply to root, no foot
summons it? Scale competing
vigour is one strength
traversed, unmet by
what departure?

a census of feet
but never due down
little 'rigour' to skimp
emulous underlay

a root no stake through foot
moves to parry the share of it
so many courses die of developing
over given steps, the crust
is grain, do as the steps dust

if the roots are *crossed*
there are no 'radical' solutions
parallel planing of feet whose
escape is mode-locked,
ultra-short dissent

roots to create (underpass)
topsoil   foot concerns
the world they did not

the heel doesn't spin nut
(rate) of a root but the
wheel between upright
and driven upon
which they are

feet unmassaged
were intention ever alone
or roots can't ditch even a plan
riser mandatory pressure
something may make them its

head-on in footsmith swing
whilst trite divisional technique
swipes the root as ornament

she was already root
her step restricted

a pace but not a stroke
when suffered to be stuck to root
arrest its licks on flux of foot

             no seeds for feet
feet not grazing above roots   root-scatter in the traction hole
sore sequences are mini-
mal freedom, tired uninsulate

piling of stones roots
kick away, used feet to,   from the befooted root
roots used to, fill that   levels out perpetual
fall into their upright,   sand, no mainlaw feet
nearest feet scavenge   but all to surfers
earth, lean room
against surface

                                  the fixed-raucous not part
                                  of part but root *to* feet
were feet roots-and?   the impro-wished way to
what could be detached   a track, poor dire
that wasn't detabled
from dance, world-
propelling branch stance?
                                  fitness of the blockage
                                  the components if moved

roots might take it
counter-urbanised,
whose cylinders and seals   root: brink them
were but soil-   end to end
loose supposings

                                  (roots)
                                  (feet)
the sect of a greeter-disorder
between the towering
and the bottomless
                                  no root gradually arrives
                                  less root than partially afoot

the frame isn't reinforced
by iteration but are there
feet as crops of the edge
snaggy with root?

vogue between their opens
excerpted closure voids

intentions scarcely fetch
between root and foot,
thoughts go on exchang-
ing customary deflections,
(vile embeddings)

feet unappreciative moving
contents, roots starve
the stored impression

the only solidarity in-
comprehensible is the step,
steps on the only
solid, root

no stream released in
break-off but clean un-
entering feet and lack
of confined wastage

erect direct as feet, are
trodden in, no matter
how unsimultaneous,
the roots keel
over and aim

feet may be a gesture
of root, the walking
not. A hesitation of
root sweeps the foot

neither foot nor root
was message: the drone of
usage was toward
incremental compound,
co-pounds a common
two-way inlet

the trail feints toward
fall of feet whereby full
into roots: feet will truck
only a laying out true

                                              bear me the way root
                                              sponges foot, each pace
feet graft roots to earth   pricks the lettings,
accord the lanes, en-   roots go waywire but
deavour the   fired into feet
cutting spares

                                              feet rest remotely, being
                                              ahead race from a
roots have scarce learning curves practice of root, no
feet all to earning cues   one step later
the store in surface proves   fasts from repose
accomplished but still runs

                                              root the accelerator, foot
                                              the zone of spread you will
                                              never set down to laid table
hard housings, from mis-take
conferring but lack
any rival, roots
may not guess the feet

                                              avoid feet/roots overt
                                              no interstices without fixation
feet from no uprising   it hardens out without
don't abandoned roots believe?   either one of them

SPACES || IN THE WAY OF FOREST

(Notations, Prevalences, Betweens)

2018

Pathless betweens no solitary dressage but pined into tall separation

if firs lean off firs they are not countervailing a forest rearing but will rake (rank) its defacing || a full plight of forest is least chasm for trees

with no issuing spatiality other than aggregation, apposition, forest result

spaces which can't be postponed even in their inert givens || at forest collide with fully operational make-way trees

a small circuit stretches into belonging (along lengths) || screened into its own spaces, events between its own orifices

whereabouts between mysterious (elongated, discontinuous) cresting || are these betweens entirely under cover?

no change of mass in the interspaces apart from falling seeds || in every nearer interval of the untorn

to say spaces in touch are climbing a trunk at a time || refining, breathing its horizontal concessions, the relinquishment entirely upright

latent spaces between where forest is abandoned, unrandomed, slyly adorned

in which there is no gradation of trees but sliding positions of a forest attending to distinctions of scope || whose adjustments are now ferried in root, unqueued as green gap

deep weather-lane into trees, a tandem to allegory || a gap gone astray but not pierced, as such remains every incomplete tree

almost a spiral of light but etiolated by gaps in the vertical, embeds a forest's exception to spread

inhabited spears of tree or small peduncles cherishing what the gaps haven't deserted || there was never any freer void to assert great surfaces of a wood run entirely through its pauses, subside as immensely relayed

cohabits forecasting woodland interval || no longer simply amid but a whole spatial weather of sheltered surface

a forest's prayerful pitch is along the interim beside it, a species out of hiding

no summitism here apart from room for empty clefts || side on side of each others' tangents of division, touch the inter-domain

small gains of copse towards every carrying passage || steep borders transmit until lightly vertical || accompany layout off the dial of the neutral

forests get supervened on, their subscenes inventories of passage minus any clear break-through || a space is not a lair, lays open how it is every envoy quietening the relay

defended but not offended at a vapour of cover || spaces suspend any alike-forest oasis of minimal (infinitive) exchange

overcome by elsewhere already overgone here, passing an intimate through an unclose

as trees puncture the open, seal its injects with denser bowers || and still the space scours, but exactly in terms of

a mass of space compromised by a missing map of trees || canopy has retextured its offload grid || space is up against (collates) its own artifices of distribution || forest rides will withhold any naturality of retribution

spaces in the forest pitch a vacant platform of duress || trees heal this distress of penetration || they lend their vertical fenestrations unaggrieved a range of dearth exceeding its depiction in trees, each departure thickens the furtherance || or nearer as an incoming of segment (place) arrives on frame, spatial shell

leeway is the frail consumer, traces assuming an advantage of covert || no entry will manage such a reciprocal exit || the way out has a longer history than passage

lanes through trees are not the forest's line of flight || set linear at integral microfret, leaves across a foiled avenue || of all places a world unhugely available || forest spaces only half-gone but entirely given on

a ground of trees in diminishing may shunt inclusion onto forest supplement || deeper incursion once branches tread into || a shelf of foliage has committed its own intersect

as if one wood could be seen from another across a paltry interval || one that leaves them both to their own convergences

what self-stealing in nature is swept up at a ruse of trees, never a single scope occupied at a time || think more of these spaces than at the full, simply pulled over forest || go sparsely into that intensity of attribution

a singular grammar of air trailing filaments || escapements of tree, busy prepositions remantling the swing of forest

dapple the forest in marginal gauze, find an antiplace ahead of ways in however thin || a whole panoply of space attends without amending, then sustains a reached fabric's no more bending

outerwise (spacing) the strong ground of a weak fulfilment, were it not for a congress of trees || puncture the layout to inhabit/venture a placing that won't overcome its betweens, its core blister of the beyond

resistance (in the way of) is a scope of completion, small pressure points that do not evacuate || spacings which inflame but do not know to excavate forest, you were never in the way as an abstainer || spaces prevent any internment but stay close to the shadows || room for mesh-like gestures are a signal for trees to begin

though spaces can be indigent, once they find themselves curved, furrowed, they will not be left naked || only the veering extent will be in borrowed clothes

spaces between trees steer at the edges and focus risings out || pinpoint ascension as spatial run-off || forest stands will offer their own denials || not taken up between

geospecific immersion (insertion) is foreign to racks of the world, but at peace between rows of trees

spacing is a curtain drawing trees closer than they could suffocate || as gaps between have the presentiment of a borderless beyond, but then a branch moves, lifts ground

margins bend their own slacker perseverance to an inseparability || o that no trees enclose themselves but only in myriad spaces of containment

few trees to affirm themselves or always in their travail of arrangement || spacings (casings) exporting forest shell

upright spaces get blown against forest, sown into cracks they clamour for the heights || storms of union, punctuated, decaptivated by a coalescence of trees

ample brace at the outset of an earth's surfaces, then trampled on until the crushed spaces ripen to forest

as nomad laces are to brambles, resident free spaces are to branches

green has three coverables: ground, branch, gap || only the one exposable: forest obstacle || adjoiningly served spine of glade

where spaces bear a rod the forest inflects the stroke, is indeed capacious foliage to be smote strong delving tracts are blind unless they circulate the frail take-up of trees | | what finally wards off sky is stealthily weak of summit

to imagine forest climax think sparsely and then space it out | | so fetch in a world overhang

a defeasibility of space is marked (uncaged) by slender trees | | rescued in the steeps to plunge anew into fellow-fractured forest

put space into forest and no further reprisals against spasmodic congress? | | no glade was ever entered post-pent

branches farm out space by dint of diminished collisions | | neither element can reform as swarm, arrives at a scarcity without deprivation

any trunk will offer its span of pre-containment | | how to plant spacings amid unsown trees

what spaces induce is a secrecy of limb | | these verticals are still in germination time with their apparency yet to be receipted

no auxiliaries (branches) without an axis of resumption | | however unrounded forest spaces stretched to access become

how tree-room finds forest flaw is beyond the mutual problematic | | a wood is no obstacle to outflow but sieves, beckons, extenuates

must these spaces always be open? | | can they sink through unbarred echoes of root? | | where space had to branch out it is no longer insolvent | | its gaps no longer need filling with forest bulk

new fellings don't clarify junctions, too wide now for spatial retry | | surfaces will be untraversable unless contaminated with forest

streams (spaces), currents (trees): a shudder of position gone behind the stem of a tree | | high forest registration, indicating the tassels in thick woods the leanest ribbons || space less wide by least asides || even dead limbs don't hang suspended but corrugate and rifle || from such a slit group let them not be disturbed in their timbers

ontological finesse (raising its own garden) stoops at forest bluster || petulant barrage, unaccomplished poles gave out the source || in which way through, what it isn't, the arbour attempts its places || vertical surroundings (not trees as soon) accompany some further portion of global reserve

if any defection *into* trees, defuses the angle of encounter at a tone of minimal reach, but given to exposure, its dimensional commons

squadrons (sweeps) in tides which a tree wades through, forest having broken onto shore

these semi-nocturnal glades better irrigate a forest in trusses than its own branch-to-branch dry channel support

live the immense limits of forest grounded in sanction of space || then see such intervals diminish themselves in order to enter || if no untainted canopy, no unassuaged shelter

little open cursus without needling forest spaces, forest depths themselves enormous in a lesser room

under best threat of all future leeway succumbing to forest zoning || at a seed-head of universal spacing

forest intervals might induce themselves treelessly || only then becoming part of a whole branch ductile

a release-stain over textures of scoured landscape || the larger the urban forest, the nearer to street it out, running green spaces into their hospital

forests between forest, unguardedly, as scarcely yarded || only a decompressor of shock betweens would have itself discarded serrieds of daily forest usage brushed into overture without surrendering the overhang

without zooming from unobstructed space where penetrated and excepted the latest prayer would not exist, rifted in the pax of adjacent finishers

between forest and its spare places is no resemblance || in contours like these offers to obstacle a coded reassembly

negative sameness of trees is positive (protective) forest equality || projective spacing, self-precipitance

if these are vertical lesions (as prayer) there are seasons of denser space by which to greet them || a between is healing their unincludeds

confined spaces can only speculate between the kinds of trees, give a species of consent to each connection

where a wood has recently been cut off spaces remain huddled || new daylight is still short on its paces || throw away an entire woodland without ghosting a single compaction of its betweens

entry a mile long kinked and knotted when it goes hard into forest without attesting

in breaks plunge amid pines like surf || I fear the last mast must be considered delayed || then comes the first intimation of a way through, where the stems thicken

stays for a dynamic of brief collateral swerve, trees behaving at their binding speed

if nothing but a desert between, a branch would still distance (instantiate) its buds, distinguish them from sheer obstacles of stretched life kindred interstices do creep but shrink from the dell | | how branches keep themselves informed, tied to the whole passenger forest

if a forest needs to get off the ground, by which to stiffen itself, it pleads spatial propensity at the roots | | intervening low density of parallel unseens

in self-retarded turn, a forest undergoes the fluents of land-locked scope, a veer at the core of root

transferred to new ground over ungraded partitions, liberates forest from its unintercepted quotient of outline | | here gaps are chipped into contiguity by every corner of tree

forest resistance: towards a broader consistency of dilation | | given the spatial take-up a way through doesn't have to resort to tree-stubble

a manifestive (troubling) through-sphere infests the trees | | then settles around blocked linears with its space in arrears, but respiring

untransportable as live forest, transmits extent by its rooted insistence | | inquisitive retentions of earth's second density

onto the precision of margins come other concise recessions | | mutually inter-penetrated but not equally interpreted

though the forest is not insulated form, it lays a seal over random passages (ravages) of earth | | out of the blockage emerges ramified flow, no more turbulent than the intersperses themselves

without confronting a retroaction of itself from the periphery, without asserting its returning outline, the forest would be at ease | | but lost amid insufficiently hindered (co-sectored) spaces

forest deals out its attachments via unlimited interior departures | | how space escapes from trees by virtue of what drains *into* cover

let these forest interspaces insist on their reversible sieve | | no hectic of release, much branch-handling of passage

the sensorium common to multiple-tree/particle-space hardly needs
a forest membrane | | or does at a moment of emitted implacable
relation

the world has been all trivial | | as well tree it or trap it, turn it loose
| | into the woods the only settled separation of nature

a shift-relation at a finite proof of forest (probing beyond its
unfinishables) is potent to root | | since outflow set a tree-mark

prayer itself an unladen space venturing between the tree-pardons
of its own pressure

where tree divides are this thin, each yields an uncertain aspect to
the other | | what might reinstate itself as thronging the same extent

as if such gaps might flatten a wood | | they *do* wrinkle into
pinpricks of ascension | | the forest is tightening its belt

if there is original forest scope, it's in not withholding a vacant
space from occupying another, not separating adjacency from the
burden of root

assembled mirage of tree/no tree nonetheless canalises at forest
fount | | best symbol gapped to a spatiality of wrap

praying the accent of overwhelmed spaces until given their
interstitial cut-out | | a forest no longer so much off its limb at this
detected labyrinth

select inflammation (vexation) at a ground of apartness *is* symbol

a speculative trial of ways-in not vanishing under woodland | |
innocent extract when employed to the difference of tree | | so
spaces don't err in their *internal* verging

less maple or willow interrogating prayer spaces than pent lanes
of fir which don't yet fully naturalise a wood | | prevents the forest
floating, offers its re-entrants

places of cut and layer but no barrage of unpinnacled wilderness | |
discrete prayer stations quietening the universals of global forest

a sapling prayer earthing up the neck of a raised root, should
pilgrimage startle the forest

take back these spaces into a tension of trees | | then do not
replicate what can't be contemplated

AS A TREE NOT A TREE

2018

If a tree is addressed not simply as the tree, but as evidence of something else, a location of *mana*, language expresses the contradiction that it is at the same time itself and something other than itself, identical and not identical. Through the deity speech is transformed from tautology into language.
              Theodor Adorno

Yet there are compelling reasons why we should not regard tautology as isomorphic—or, worse still, identical —with identity, the full extent of which may even have escaped Adorno himself.
                 Ewan Jones

And still we have not
spoken
of
non-roots
    Jan Erik Vold

1

A tree has its not-tree
range, strange burial
of no further form

can a tree substitute
itself as what it
isn't, by ways
it is?   at tug of
condensed steepage

less what isn't yet a
tree but at its
scarcity tailing
relative recess,
amended to be
not as a tree
might cease to be

at no-one's tree, had
about its edges least
vestige, that slight
congress of hyper-tree

2

Trees frailer than self-
invention, but not an
untree despite woods
settling counter to all
landscape appurtenance

lets trees visibly
partake of their broken
(stem-targeted) quantum

a not-tree assays few
lamentations of outcome,
in pact with its
branch-laying horizon

3

Grounded over-goodly in
upstabbings of ground,
how a tree will rise
into its mode (not
stood but reared)

as the cope is own-
host intuition, shelters
what it is not. Closer
to a resistance
than any further stop

4

Tree of what has been
differently given, not
riven in difference:
lateral shoots from how
sorely (solely) a tree

tools for it amid
a pool of roots, proto-
fabric but still to
awn over what is
intimacy its own
but not itself

tree not tree in a
paradisal escapade of
symbolic compaction,
clenches what dispenses,
shares and craves out

5

A tree's face at stoodness
imparting, non-tree in-
variance simplifies similars
of forest departure

not as scowl but through
distributed face scrawls a
more deferent range of the
not, needy for gapped
(unslipped) envelopment

trees will sufficiently
bother (untether) the ground,
its call towards no further
cells of root declension

6

Not-tree (shafting) is the sift
of tree to its wealth, its
gulf in spate of itself

branches reproved for their
recondite nests, twists a
nothing which insists on
fathomed instep, upwind of
tree blown towards bower

they need to be taller
than their seed in re-
making a tree, lift at/
through the seams of
nearest apart-from

together trees imitate
contrary content no more
than merely, incite every
branch to a population

7

Trees hewn down or further
than ever from sporting
opposite savour, lack of
tree-verticals percolates
these post-composites

or tree-flack was the
first of fired deposits,
slakes the thirst for
parallel crushed merits

preventing a tree en-
dows it with an echoic
saliency, leans against
such and such a
non-aggregate

8

Opens a tree too pendant
for non-tree run-off,
roots levelling trunk
in no further display
than mantle

erectless from amputation,
a dispute facility with
branch continuation, rare
trees when a not-tree pacifies
the turmoil, parallel
gift insistence

abrogation of counter-
fronds to a more punitive
sustenance, newer forms
than any difference

the space of non-tree
perfectly embodies
the petition towards

9

Rudiments of self-cancellation
to assort trees one another
beside others more than
themselves, how non-tree
averts any hulk crew
of borrowed resistance

enterprise of postings
not just latent tree-
thinnings, the non-tree
stands large in the plea
of its quasi-organs

strands across the gift
continuum, as such rather
focused rampage, what a
non-tree is not
putting into the void

10

Tiny hooks of proto-
consonance, milder
belonging to differential
sequence, dense with an
offered lessening of connection

nil participation without pre-
cipitating (lignifying)
what a tree isn't

a tree doesn't brace
itself, no need in the
fate of simpler absences
between itself
and erasure

non-tree won't steal the
ground but stealthily
wields it, neither
was it an explorer

11

Tenderly defected from, but
trees' nearest style in tree,
their inhabitative denial

tree/non-tree the only
cleavage must be
vertical, there is no
ontological thievery

simply group trees trans-
natal to woodland,
their so awkward down-
draft from assarting

12

Become less than what
they aren't, trees with
multiple sights across one
espial, this they have
the shade for

reciprocal exception tree
from tree evenly a contrary
exemption, never so
lightly fallen across
tree universals

otherwise-than-tree alike,
bespoke clamorous woodland,
its recoil escapes the spike

inner forest dissension,
don't rest on a half
-tree but its relief from
a next to tree:
entire rank in counter-
angle of treeless intimates

13

What is given trees, now
dryly a core-wood,
each ample wrinkle
cuts aslant to grain
but brittles further off

at a tree's negative
no inversion, just a sym-
metrical cancellation
shadowed across the
same changed field

not at-tree in further
forest, no such homing
as tree-mass, lonely
decisions of proximity

14

Scission not an obscurity
of tree to itself but sheered
collaborative glade, the
effects of canopy over
what branchings themselves
never conspire to

take a tree to know
not-a-tree via its
volition of reception,
no passive or vacant
after-effort

a nothing of tree shouldn't
revisit its provision but
does go further than
parallels of revision

15

Trees resume forest, an
accord they are minus a
claim, unaiming but
assentingly staged

machine acutes be-
stride ecological blunts,
what trees pose to each
other in that mode,
their ingrown fissures
insult no calmer
wooded interim

a tree not its own
not, fully alongside
eventful disanimations,
induration grants
inaugural tree-storm,
recommends clamouring for norm

16

Oughtn't to pursue rigid
self-loss, given a non-
tree readily intertwines,
dipping leaves onto
original unbare branch

touch of not a tree
milder than its lesion
divines, holiness of through-
forest, patience to
branches of obstruction

unavailable forest origin
a tree's path of prayer:
no livable disinheritance
not already adoration

17

With tree no tree, so less
than is owed alterity, the
scarcity accelerates elision
towards collision by encumbrance

going through a larch but not
abstracting it from trees,
press on arborescently from
what it is most not

what trees wanted to discard
didn't unplug the earth,
green parts couldn't contrive
premature pallor, spindleless
but no other spine in season
apart from vertical trial

wrong no's fall as seeds
and hides, singing in secret
host to a tree without throes

18

If not a tree then rinsed
in deep tackles of what
unblanks branch, this is
ontological filter accumulating
residue, a rubble of
cranked (returned) residence

few roots within such a tree-
wise likelihood of forest
rotation, fantastically
thicketed to the very dearth
of the universe: prayer
plus a tree of its gainsay

if all trees were one tree,
how ungreeted a tree would be

if not-trees were the only tree,
how nodeless they couldn't brave to be

GIVEN TREES
THEIR OTHER SIDE OF NATURE

2019

It was as if suddenly imperceptible vibrations had been transmitted to him from within the tree; he was set against it without a care, so that nothing else was visible… making an effort, he strenuously wondered what had happened to him… had he got to the other side of Nature?

Rilke, *Erlebnis*

The other side of nature is the side that allows it to be more than… our own production. The other side is the side that we sense but do not see, that is turned away from us toward that distance from whence it is rendered, out of which it is bestowed, and to which—retaining a certain fidelity—it inclines.

Bruce V. Foltz

I could not find a privacy
From Nature's sentinels—

Emily Dickinson

1

Beside a tree, rest its parts against a tangle of rotation, its horizon-pedal   oblique lunge but slender launch, non-severance of a spared-across

Woods keep apart other seams for briefer slivers   then to be entangled in sluggish leaf, anchored at tree-shavings

        crossing the woods
        in a mobile
        storage of us

        not fending off
        arboreal hearsay
        but a gentled
        clod of leaf

Is prescience the first to cloud over, discover opacities conjoined in leaf?   naturals feeling (not peeled by) their other grade (guide), performance in sheaf?

Prayer not bridging but a thrown (penetrated) embankment, its own least-beyond from-which   whose humped bends can be as forward as they are

2

A tree's future into nature or furtive for its other side   sheer of furthers, the para-nurture, at tree-entry's praying stride

A clotted fountain spitting tree, flits across rampant idling of the not-yet-sown   how nature swings through one final reversion from what it hadn't simply grown

        woods emptied at
        their other side of
        gift, fills itself
        into the filmic
        density

        shoot controlled woods
        onto their pivot
        jerking a prayer's
        reclusive hinge,
        effusive range

        a tree's own
        as if unblown
        other side to
        nature, roots
        presaging re-
        visionary seed

The vehicle's beached ship of woods navigates its longest journey abed   how roots roam projections, the vessel overladen is all green protection

If earth isn't thwarted it turns as the trees turn   forays of arboreal poverty capacious entering elements (spun entanglements)

3

Flattened forks of a stubble tree, is it open or not?   how many instalments are there to its awkward (entrenched) widening?

Every (invisible) phase of tree is completely applicable   if merely a fluid in flux, then not yet installed in a stance that pleats the visible which is usable prayer

    human trellis
    of a tree, its
    spiritual continuum
    bounces the span
    of the initial
    resonance's
    counter-proposal

    what the other
    side of nature
    asks *of* nature,
    scarcest nurture
    at the horizon tree

    minor branching
    to divest tidal
    earth, nature
    has that minimal
    inland sea

Woodland seized out of cloud, escapade in perpetual brim slashed onto root   things become the incident of their ontological ramming, prayers of occluded (applied) ramification

Hasn't turned without reverting to burden, pulsing a symbol drag so much lighter than any mustered growth, simply the reliance itself

4

The other side of nature a dearth between depths, provisional tree-shadow of the unconditional, steep liturgy of arousal   green filigree fasting off global shelter

It might allay the glance of trees, no other side of nature that needs *pounce*, the enhancement is the beckoning itself   gains corrugation in trunk, shelfless unless amid counter-branching

                expected (unattended)
                trees, does as its
                other side, what
                coincides at the
                foliage frequency

                upper and lower
                identities of its
                limitation,
                other-worldly
                warmholes

Within the vertical other, not behind   without any containing unless it (lengthily) swivels, so gift particles revive in getting to grit the turn

To the other side of nature, not a resilience but a conciliation no naturals can morph, trees at their weaker ascensions

5

As if under a disempowering tree, nature avoids annulling the alarm
  no beechwood will call out so blondly again   the sole side trees can practise until horizon offers a still paler, the one side which does specify tree-group to the real

The eventual holy by which trees trouble nature   long foliage of ontological assay, at last face-side-up for spontaneous delay

                trees at unreasonable
                union, buoyancy traps
                (sweeps) leaf, scarcity
                reseals, nature re-
                scales (sets source
                from its meta-curdlings)

                no reverse facia
                but a tree en-
                twined, grained by
                passages lost
                apart from attach-
                ments, striations

Woods had long desisted their frame, other-siding nature shares (resorts to) its scarcity in similars

As a tree will mirror nature's other side, too stretched for alternative visibles (gift-sites) but leaf-veined onto the reflection

6

Stunt to spare surfaces like a local norm, won't dress the given shadow
   let nature's other side take to the etiolation, its converse universal
network until sheer plant filament stretches inclusion to its outright

As a fox will fathom a forest from fierce fastenings, as such already
within paddings of horizon, exposure to no further insistence   drag-
marks haven't shifted but transfer alliance, motion of what needed to
prove it probed

                   trees are plants
                   to the event, other-
                   flanked without
                   derision, coastal
                   where it drains on
                   infinite distance

                   ask trees for their
                   belonging-towards
                   as birds take off
                   from leaf before branch,
                   the immediate quake

Multiscalar then gusted onto the shell of trees   woodland mesh
unruffled by what it doesn't have (what it hardened) being what it
does   stagnant but lignant enough to connect to gift reserve

Arboreal disposition (prevalent woodland) doesn't need to disparage
other sides of gift (little grafted as such) since no prime materials are
simply for loan

7

Not everything crosses a tree with life   the side of nature it doesn't have isn't now alone with itself but is nearest prone

Earth how far, pummelled at soft-veined doors   will only centre on tree-stamina once it surfaces encrusted, scraping adaptive spoors

        a country of woods
        the faltered deposit,
        othergates beside

        roots won't mangle
        inherence for cusps
        of opportunity, not
        yet entanglement
        until slender ob-
        stinate ratification

        obstruction is for-
        warder than it
        flares out
        traversals

The other side by which gift-destination knows this tree-speared side was never isolated because in shelter of its pre-unique location

Nature's other side no less born, sensory only as its gift bestirs   a fragility not quite nearby but companionate burden

8

Greennesses facing semi-soluble flow, blanker side tidal only at the roots   while leaves surge up their summit pools, woodland precipice

No expense of reserve that couldn't arise nakedly as world   a leaf garners any counter-slide until naturals by gift breathe their one other side

        pale periphery
        in trust of
        prominent tree,
        one other spring
        set back

        porously relays
        through a
        brittle filter its
        unlosables,
        reducibles

Trees alive, resolves well past their parkland   only such fugitive bands might have thinned enough   nature's further side a rail to its adjunct once again

Overtaking green with unseen array and hold   nature reserves its lessers for a rarer take which won't be slighted, the weather-side of gift

9

Lest gift be any looser than a seized drift, finds its guide at blocked tree-traces, packed easier that way to horizon

No such erasure without a raised other side, what is not a lid
    hidden only as leanness against, supportive until obstructive
enough for prayer

                    unfeeling wood
                    but knowing
                    by country
                    its obverse side,
                    unreversed
                    dalliance

                    traps a summer stick
                    bulging with
                    winter into spring
                    as spent leaf-
                    display burns its
                    fossil in the mesh

                    nature's is the
                    universal charred
                    (carried) bush

Less fear of bruised asides once nature's closure is double-entry branches all registers of the mutating surround

The fallacy of blankly seeing past instead of the immediate vasts, they also jog the estate: here woodland mediates a far-sided sprawl, inveterate brow

10

A leaf can't unlearn windings of a fresh nature's counter-turn   horizon would be a spindle only unless braked among trees clustering their faith in a meta-rotation

Nothing is stripped by a damaged absolution   trees will never simply hang off horizon but prove as nature's other side does

> rootedness scratches
> at a dimensionless
> deflective abiding
>
> in welts of belonging
> the unaccountable,
> prongs of the trees
> smack at nature's
> reserve
>
> the tread of a
> leaf to earth
> pawed at its
> printway

As if a tree's other side weren't a prodigy, but its compounded covering offence   scouring one face doesn't handle the neck of it, nothing of a given trembles as contrary

Take these worn possessives to truth's extra room (equalised compression), scant *with* prayer's compatriot assembly

11

A wood's gone trailing coned from root   unspurned but waiting for its nether face among the post-naturals

Riven from trees their nature's other speed, unhesitant root   where a spinney troops to communion, heavy with not yet ventured calluses

>   nature's rind
>   lifts off
>   two-sided
>   necessities
>
>   or a collision
>   of pine opens
>   like a cone
>   missing its
>   curb
>
>   routines of
>   gift owing
>   the new hand-
>   icap of prayer,
>   lenient to
>   leaf among the
>   bending co-
>   consternations

Blurted slipways unbinding but slackening differentially through forest   against such trunkage ontological invasion is double-sanded, root-rubble provided

Rucks raggedly across the other side of nature   porous externals in poorer folds deprived of any provisional opposition to gift

SKIES IN FLIGHT OF TREE

2019

We are mistaken… if we expect to find in prayer a shelter from the overwhelming force of mystery. It is… in prayer that we will cease to perceive this mystery as the distant horizon of our human sensitivity and begin to hear about ourselves in the encompassing challenge.
JOHANNES METZ

But then be careful not to drain away the contents of the *object* (clouds), not to take it, any longer, initially, in its evidentness, not to use it any longer… except *allegorically*.
PIERRE CHAPPUIS

   as sky and trees
      repeat leaves in flame
             on the other side of a flight path
ZOË SKOULDING

1

Sky in breadth but no range in store, moreover there are trees
   narrow assistant tallness, poplars wedge a sky's suspense

As skies drum onto land they bounce off horizon   the shock is
trees absorbing (rescaling) the derision

          find adjacent
          filter: one telescopic
          flown speck is
          another haven
          speckled

          earliest ascension
          was sky in trunk,
          not yet peeling
          the earth

          from one spurt
          (foliage) to another,
          the hurt is sky
          not yet in grain
          for launch

Headless stalks are no better prickles before windowless sky
   streak it along a tree's brushway for actual take-off

Rarely at any world-search, the sky flies through it   then dived to
see how wingless in leaf it was

2

All over brief earth the heavens are secondary soil   trees assist it
with aileron, one flap a no longer grounded rotor

Curtained round mute shell, a thin fusilage from disaster
  wingless before the heavens' own dispelling fabric

                tenting its
                ground, the forest
                frets itself
                vertical, no sheer
                skyplay then

                let sky waters pre-
                serve a forest's
                own tidal

                sky-dismantled
                oak moving like
                a tuft of cloud

A lesser into flight   woodland perfections obtain the poor-floor of
that soaring

Havens at corner-stops, struts for any sky-bearing flight   nurtured
surfaces on universal glide

3

Woodland mirage of terrestrial fluttering   only quiet roots become aligned with their hollow gutters, strict matters of sky

Adversary skies not accusative but resort to nominal forest: innocent of material they cloak a sum of horizon which lets leaf risk them over   shelter by traversal threads

        forest haven
        grows ravenous
        unless it taper
        sky off a body

        a warren of trees
        least queasy
        barrenness from
        digesting sky

        until the crowns
        tilt (disenmesh)
        what they rotate

Tree a living abject readily overflown   or a comet to a bush, hovers the gloom it expels

New clouds over fusiform hurdles, only a sky could leap this wooded recession   lift from the attrition but never become its own vehicle

4

Carbon bunches reseeding the sun across its sky semi-dust   haven flotsam preinjected at tree level

Unhoused in air but as free forest afloat   skies of adjacency no longer trivial dispensers overhead

>
> not yet a tall
> bend in forest,
> does make us
> twist (not test)
> the heavens
>
> unclotted sky
> new woodland
> rinses it
>
> less abutment
> above unless
> excerpted
> in trees

The fleeting bearing of tree sessions (seasons) breeding (swooping) the sky   let it be in loft

Vertebrae by which the heavens flock back to themselves   not instructed but trusted on distended root

A woodland will sow steep pasture (sky) along its after-root summits

5

A ridge bristling in spruce   needles massed against weightless
flight in what propagates (turbo-vents) *positions* of flight

Hovering like a no longer reeling beyond   betweenness mid-sky,
granted its horizontal graduals of ascent

        air-worthy in
        festoon, tree
        mass dissolves
        cloud morass

        if predominance
        of air then domes
        of forest, commons
        in steepage

        launch (lunge)
        its span, filter-
        wards to
        horizon

Where trees are hooded they parachute a sky gate-crashing earth
  at which uncrowned heavens billow out again

Horizon as carrier (encounter) will encircle only as forest pressed
lobes to the sky

6

Havens can accuse skinless sky now the earth is no longer naked
   and forgive forced flight continuing across leaf acceleration

Trees post-naturals even to their plantation ribs, upbribed bones
   which does rob skies towards further participation in the unfolding

                a tree blooms
                its sphincter
                of air, alert
                sky-tail

                prayer of the heavens
                for lading, on hold
                not dropped
                where dipped

                in luminous
                trench, outflown
                by what it
                retains

Visit the undrowned joinery of this spinning branch as it corrugates its sky, propels encompassing

Azure at a crust of horizon, dried precipitation doing the rounds of earth limitation   in sky of this very projection

7

Insufficiency of sky, so much beyond forest but not yet in flight
  zoneless prayer

Impossible to renaturalise forest once it's *this* poplar to indifferent
heavens: no longer a focal layer, given the transitional fixture   or
makes out local prayer

                skies endless at
                lesser ends of tree,
                co-versions, elated
                scouring

                with wind sonics
                lulled after-
                mirages of a windlass
                sky hauled
                offshore

From innate poverty (forest) towards pinnate promptitude   a sky
winged (the wound scarcely) by trees of its amplitude

Tree taper for an ecstatic unshearing   within woodland density
skies are no longer super-immense, simpler congruent   the
current isn't equivalence but prayer

8

That a tree will sky-sail on its root pitch   green pads for unmoving (fully transferable) launch

Postnatural by gust of reception, immersive though not absorbtive
    prayer its own counter-surplus, difference comes to carrying a sky by tree

        inner truism of
        forest temptation
        from within its
        non-desert

        tree dependence
        (skies) rarely a
        portable label,
        over-attached
        unless prayed

Brittle heavens can't coalesce the nearer intention   stretch it to trees, they then devote a release   prayer's unplanned precision

When trees will absorb surface, a sky is no longer reduced to its peak   these owings are prayer's own

9

How roots squeeze earth to embolden trees, skies for the welling of it   touch prayer at the two inflecting loose ends

Telescopic texture is pine raising its flying by ground   how they protect sky specifics   prayer needling reception, shared foreshortening

        decimated passage
        as sky makes height
        from trees, they
        rally its lift

        azure from a
        quarry of
        shadow kept
        bright at
        stroke of branch

        to leap itself
        highly, how
        sky remains
        in veil risen
        aground

Formless sky not skipping its tree-stiffening   then let it scope every other sycamore body

Trees don't coat the heavens, simply elongate them   reach is no longer a forest home but the flight medium is

Sky/trees: a paradox if deliberate renaturalism is squarely a surplus of horizon   flight the property of one, the body of another   prayer's reinventive   secure scarcity of vertical attendance

A poverty of risen sky treads out its face at the foot of trees   then takes on the branched apparatus (flight), among wings of the greener apparency

        not forest garden
        but freely occurred to
        skies which ride
        the earth once astride
        it tree-shapen

        already surpass
        super-travelled
        across these fabric
        speeds of tree

Parallel days of forthcoming   a sky braided with all it can't float   as these backings intend, allegorical (hinter-matter) transfer

Trees a gatekeeper to sky? no, but its breathable admittance   as nodal the membrane is foliar sediment, not emissive demarcation

A riddle of sky from middle forest, a network concussion among flying paddles   given that woods have sustained their own jetwork, loan it to the sky's ramped beginnings

11

Where a plantation overgrows its floor (by interior obstruction) it knows which flight compensation litters the sky

Glides the reference across skyables of tree inference   obstruction not on these lengths occlusive

> air within the
> silences of a
> wood can only be
> salient, habitual
> sky promont-
> ory, no other
> harness
>
> as sky isn't thrown
> from trees to be up-
> hurled, *is*
> outcurled
>
> a ground's deed,
> to be skied-
> out by root

As aching rootstone will sky-front its pulled lever   forests can't right themselves unless yoking the heavens into flight

Once among the skies of their carriage, root ballast does fully respire, won't retract

Oblique forest overtly flying the sky   hyper-scanning the limits to any disappearance onto root

12

On skyroads (larch forest) the heavens cross themselves   flight is from the ground up   redress at a co-extrusive blessing

A nape of sky draped across, shoulders minus any climb to limb
   it grows dark once forest has surrendered the daily flight-zone canopy   vertically but never sequentially aboard its own aerial delegation

                 less dendritic bridges
                 than what trees
                 allege of sky

                 earthmost body
                 in tree, grows
                 flightsome, sees
                 its chosen density
                 encourage skies

                 branches no longer
                 shredded once sky
                 shapes across
                 flown (frayed)
                 edges

Clarities above once cleared of trees   sky can't wipe the floor with them until exact tree-line has flown it apart

Hacked to a wide strip of naked vertical sky   set trees to reappear above it, delve it into flight

BODIES THE TREES OF

2019

For J.H. Prynne, who gave me a copy of my leading source

Some Sources

Claus Mattheck & Helge Breloer, *The Body Language of Trees: a Handbook of Failure Analysis* (1997)
Lisa Robertson, *Cinema of the Present* (2014)
John Kinsella, *The Wound* (2018)

Through trees of it over again   towards their bodies of   tallest free-standing despite heavy offloadings   hostile time given a life too long for its wait in trees   if branched, straining at the waist of   world body abroad of tree, at its boardings vertical

Particles of the earth's body at a further remove in trees   split beams leafing through to an unknown mechanism of reaction   crisp diagrams in the faces of   cracks radiate, the root-swerve revolves   describes (sub-writes) a blow   stronger ribs of woundwood will tissue its stricken foam

Wound spindle, then enlarges context zones   unless the compensatory fibre buckles more casually in the future   a hazard beam solidly informs (infirms) displaced wood fibres   conversion of body to body, less need of tree intervals   trees liable for a break before they fall promptly, the soil has no such leisure   buckle before they shear, push emergency growth onto its lee side

Outspread whether slipped or not is ontological transition   recoded from its nub, ontological transmission   resorts to world according to a snapped limb, ontological trans-section   how trees actualise their hazard   silent signs render screams to seams

Close a wound too rapidly and lightning internal cracks will feel the start   foliage alternately stripping/ripening the axiom of stress in tree uniform   comparative rarity on site with minimal material expense   discarding its collar before hazarding

A stress dispersal in uniform drift   until leafing sports the wind from tusk to tree-root, shirkers of structure, underloaded under a load that will stretch it   long lever arm, inverse furtherance springs up at wind/wood contact   a notch tailored toward a void of stress, leans into its own gathering semi-crescent

Interweaving up to its weak point, a junction between sunlight and lateral forking   failure along a defect-free stem, the fibres kink junctionwards   shortcomings in trees: wood can't remould itself except with superfluous reinforcement   excessive stalling into shape   trees share horizons of the body across all the unsheltered flesh of the world

From solid cylinder (trunk) to wooden stems hollowing stems of common signature   trees to the lesser dispensation, universal access   hollow tree, from closed shell onto disseminated fracture-planks   oaks bundled onto their statues   not before demonstrating available shoulders for bodies still surfacing

What camber build did now a freedom treed it   the flotation hovers over a least bloated (fertile) standing   once a trunk becomes a body it's no longer made of turntables   swivels from break to creakage, rakes an axle horizon but holds to a world arising from freak rigidities   cementing a populated tableland where the wizened greenery super-consists, most loanable limbs patiently intact

The city has a right to restore you in little takes, new bark noses over its buds   branches in harness, propping, towing, a whole people's fleshless infilling   universal fibre transfer   the trepidation not of branch-body but of abstract city   untranslatable once there is no further urban weight-loss

A pine tumbling into cones   its removable bodies are the pebbles roots fork through   no pine climbs the winter night except in retaining its range, its ascendant proto-footing   recurs (coagular scission per session) in the smallest possible spruce accident

Until earth can schematise beyond the surface engineering of trees   it curves before horizon, they truncate an above or below   crash rather than not make a redivision loudly coincide

Good-natured relations, failure progresses to its open cavities   the little 'legs' of a hollow stem carrying nature's kinks sideways   abrupt infusion from cavities to solids   black squares of shelter-ferment

Even a recumbent stone can provoke a nodule step from a tree   wrapping corrugations perform a reaction bolus as their primordial project   axial jags can only mount the buttress at a waiting for the stem to return

A tree is undone like a rope untwisted but no such removal of swerve from world   unanchors a wood-stripe above the wound, a tree's integument of universal body   any generic body recognises its fibrous source, its abrasive allowances   a helical fracture face, yawns across collective lithe bodies   skeletal advice for lending out

Always such fidgeting (forest profile) at the bends and twists in bodies to be exchanged: nature blocks a mocking tree, then embodies it   ruined world but perfectly betokened, limbs are lent its walking across astounded

No ground fiction can render the boundary of a root-ball even   pressures share out a world asymmetry across uncompensated particulars   prayer the singular addition until each layering echoes universal membrane

Nature's failure rate travels some way up the stem of the world   it is trees thrashing at the same ways of bodies   there will be no coarsening of each other's storms but there will be external tender coatings allaying the immovables   is the country you are restrained at a something become, one out of tree?

Such a distribution must be stretched round more than animal bodies   plenitude needs the special observance of tree-strain, its grainy latitude   we do everything with our bodies that branches might stand us for

The beeches, heavy prone, haven't lapsed into their deservances, they take on the demerits of prowling limb   embossed at tiny bracts of revival, this body appoints its swelling zone, compelling a remedial take-up of advisory flesh   tree-grudge gives us the spirit, corporeal intricacy festooning its risers to a roller canopy, transduce the friction

No universal body apart from what stems at buckling   the only comparison a tree wears: body narratives run through a plant seam which the trees take taller, inclusive induration broadcasts its matrix, net the gaps and reassign the verticals   universal manners of slighted allness

If a tree, a crane to so many other bodies, micro-pulleys along shareable fibres   macro-tunnels of observant diversity   slight enough to enliven the danger points of stunted torsos at folds of donation

A tree is all the issues of a frame exploded onto branch   the body's polemics acutely static, across which wind-rock becomes another translating limb

The only gatherable lives go via a tree's pact with induration   theirs is the upstanding between, what there is for a borrowed limb to rear

Loaded green repose just to this side of any innocent bodily location   no dirt of incorporation deceiving trees, this is their transmissible shape going for adoption   usually a merciful horizon has been fought over a tree's body

An essential spiritual poise (chosen) at the tree's involuntary bent elbow   given to world arises from a living collar callusing a riven at world   actual distribution texture in the rind of a trunk

To world bodies at large a tree isn't an interval but a sentinel bowing over bestow a form   consulate woodland in its capacity paucity, generic planetary revision   so-called earth as stretched to trees, barer patches might have seen other rare plants

A gate makes it into a copse, a branch body moved it from where it stood   minimal contact area, the makings of local description   colludes with bending loads, to simulate an entry's own trial of reaction wood

A sociability of arboreal transforms, one parabody at a time   strange physical trade-offs overtook the foliage   raw payout in the pockets of trees   only the strictest physical samples (coinage of body imitation) can make that a thicket for world

From nature's dark relations through to natural shading bodies   second-growth forest re-tempers its third age limbs   a tree knee for across-species sponsorship   an animal entering a field is a forest distended beyond yield   makes an archway towards its mammalian branch

A multitude of small animals recites the limbs of trees   it is their own limbs entering the wood, such wider practices of fibres in a truss   the time of forest speculation is a rooted spider-ant all over its surfaces

Calling sooner than new limbs down on the treeless   disparate bodies will no longer echo inferential roots but also hold discarnate any *burdenless* novelty of surface   the splinter-habit shedding branches is arms/legs animating an escape into shape-likeness

Anyway up, any fresh carapace, a tree-filler's earth of trims   walk away, legs go branchiform, caress common bodies into a travel without departure

A lone tree the pure flesh of its post   bodily evidence at world posting   sifting blown wreckage for a tree diagram, at horizon's own extremity a new diaphragm   to explore world organs at a metaphysics of tree

A body won't stay where a tree squats over its pinpoint limb   however much exact positioning is sitting on a branch

A gap in the planet baled out by tree-pumps   in our bodies the clotted city, copied tendrils angling at rather than with trees   finger-bone or arm-like, the toggle clasp of towards or from

It wasn't bowers gave a planetary physics of tree   only its broadness from a brashing of arc, the bristling   body ramification which filters animate becoming   combing inslant surpluses, *ie* beams bent off tree

SNAG OF A TREE

2020

In memory of Benita Parry

It is this whole field of the 'vertical' that has to be awakened…What is upright is the existence that is threatened by weight, that leaves the plane of objective being, but not without dragging with it all the adversity and favours it brought there.
MERLEAU-PONTY

    never nothing quite
        ending ever, after
   every intervention
            protection

HARRIET TARLO

Note

In this context, a 'snag' is an upright dead tree left to withstand/decompose naturally in the midst of a forest.

1

Standing in full forest   at the ruin of a tree every disadvantage bar one   is the one it is gives   too stiff for thriving   its super-added givens

Indurate flesh vertically porous   at a puncture the call of hyper-commonality   so long as the ruin stands   opaque pylon, obstinative cipher

> Destitute boundary
> not fallen on itself,
> broad branching as
> death's surrogate
>
> a silent world ladder
> no horizontal support,
> unconditional rung
> teeming stiff, a
> rigor vitae
>
> forest being woody
> comes at this knock:
> abandoned form
> a hollow cage to
> symbolic refit

Uprights at the rate of ruin, crammed wellsprings of   from loud cavity to the silent hollow prime decay releases expressly at the tip   the blunt grip as much as tapering

No direct apology for rigid tendrils in this barbarous wood   presses an age-scorched lignum onto its rocket nervure   on upreared surface   arrest at a new pool

2

Calcified tree-flesh risen perched dead into locus   brief re-creation in post-complete stasis   no other reprisals at the blockage

Dehiscence a dried-up vertical tense of a time   ruin a tensile pillar continuing to (not with) indifferent scatter   exhausted future fabric at its incoming mooring

                Effect a decaying to
                new origin, posted
                  at the afterlife
                  (counter-spring)
                    of upsurge

                a having-been at
               its vertical retake,
                    site-specific,
                   brittle-pacific

              sufficient density to
               taper own sediment,
               alignment passes its
               sway, becomes manifold
            (solitary) accompaniment

A reject accorded physiognomy, a cast of the wiles of crumble-shot carbon   post-sentience is last to be fully sited   winking the follicles of removed foliage

Unwrecked ruin too late for its horizontals, its feeding trail from wider tedding   the vertical snag deposits present non-conditions as offer   a dead upright replies to its latent knowledge

3

Snag on tree suspends its temporals, hung at post-   frozen into
a diverted (chosen) currency of wood   naked delay has become
newest lateness, forest internal bridge

The gamut broached through its sole fixed (unlistless) object
   whose snagged moment is vertical ruin crossing the one thing
it offers   from immersion towards its deathly non-extinct para-
envelope

             Siphoned whirlwind
             not removed but thinned
             to be the place of,
             hook, snare, vertical peg

             disintegration a crystal
             between moment blocked
             by moment

             statics enrol a pin
             in a confluent stammering
             forest, punctual at its
             symbolic interim

A destruction vest gives the attestation   onto the difference of its
own atemporal explosion   ruin resorts to time as obstructed
plant the grit instancing its prowess, seizure on behalf of counter-
contour proffering forest

A dead upright the move from subsistence towards existence   its
persistence a full fuel intermediate and not only where the gift of it
is   a woodland's self-delaying (praying) institution

4

The Tree's ruin a farther defection   newest before reflect-layers of horizon, the having-been at a not yet seen

Frozen into a hesitation post-ultimate friable with age   weakness of life at its prominent verticals   a poverty placates the transfer, sub-replete, super-complete

>   The weight of dropped
>   core at its slender
>   formals, become own snag
>   doesn't hover or cover
>
>   beckons its unflown
>   rig, towards uprights
>   taller than drag
>
>   as post-temporal
>   rent eternally, not
>   that it fails to shunt,
>   digesting a tree at its
>   life-lock, root-rock

A coming to be as stands to relations of its becoming, the difference of prayer within one of these further post-serial folds, the crackle of obsolete limb

Lateral transcendence offered a dead frontal vertically on behalf of
    alert to the prop's post-allergy, the taper signals upwards of strain in gift among its livid swellings

5

A maiming (sans alteration) toward the same prescient latency   a ratio not sustainable by vitality alone   now only the verticals stay on, pure upshot raft of sediment

Injured space within standing relief   from the promiscuity of woodland towards this indication   imbricates at a stagnant resonant post   as transform much the least transfer

> Let a forest stab
> its own timber-yard,
> vertical stores, silica-
> wood rooted in
> stony standing
>
> truck with the unfallen
> waiting to slip its
> side-limb, at snag
> nothing like a cross-
> section, proffers horned
> vertical access
>
> a prayer-perch at
> an after-pause of
> layered vitals, circular
> life round a stop
> stripped to prop

A banished temporal knows its rib slower than life, time's scaled (indurate) after-flow   only at snag are givens scorched into by release-decease, no longer peeling from seepage

Arrest at a stubbed toe of forest, the disjoint is what it achieves in tow   traction only from where a snag sticks

6

In the office of undoing, no preface of unmaking   only a
reattribution (the lack of stagger) at an indivisible liminary shake
obdurate transfix rugged enough for raising the altar zoning

At a basement of time in outright casement, poverty's open dart
the snag as a post-model timber, a spear stuck on horizon

            Tree snags per
            acre is stillage
          for hollow cavities,
           wildlife-leafless

           hard snag its own
          heart-rot navigates,
         sumptuous plateaux
         amid the dead of life

      homes surrendering their
     domes for a larger vantage
           of the undowned

Snag proclamation on the same side as its death   the relegated
pillar a whole forest stalks, its free-tree broken off in mid-pause

Satisfies its order from the foot of surface disturbance, verticals
emergent with subsiding: fully a moist mast on the brink of being
asked the way   not yet recanting the chinks of its signal

7

Awarded incongruent its counter-start, a no longer life-loaned full participation   at a stub of forest pivotal target, packed across prayer

Snag as active duct, its due inclusive take-out from life   non-neutral complicity, post-alive simplicity

        Initialled stick of a
        seedling below, to be
        under a vertical vest,
        through its life a
        post-mature stake

        reversal over-pins
        a generous bleakness of
        snag, tell all-up to site

        now in time to be only
        partially what it became,
        particles taller than
        each other alive

What things were there at point of being by snag to it, the prayed of   no ontological wrangle splinters onsite inseparative crumble

Givens at their refreshed vertical rasp, corrosion offers outcome a core of its broadcast: snaggle of tenets, stag furniture

www.ingramcontent.com/pod-product-compliance
Lightning Source LLC
Chambersburg PA
CBHW031159160426
43193CB00008B/438